Kīlauea
The Newest Land on Earth

The summit of Kīlauea with Mauna Loa in the background.

Bishop Museum Special Publication 92

Kilauea
The Newest Land on Earth

Photographs by Dorian Weisel
Text by Christina Heliker

Bishop Museum Press

Honolulu

1990

"Jets of lava sprung hundreds of feet into the air and burst into rocket-sprays that returned to earth in a crimson rain; and all the while the laboring mountain shook with Nature's great palsy, and voiced its distress in moanings and the muffled booming of subterranean thunders."

Mark Twain, Roughing It

© 1989 by Bishop Museum
W. Donald Duckworth, Director

Note: Unless otherwise indicated, photographs in these pages are by Dorian Weisel and are from his personal collection. Dorian Weisel holds copyright to his photographs that appear in this volume.

BISHOP MUSEUM PRESS
Post Office Box 19000-A
Honolulu, Hawaii 96817

Designed by Gerard A. Valerio

Printed by Toppan Printing Co., Japan

Library of Congress Catalogue Card No. 89-082088
ISBN 0-930897-46-3

Many people have contributed to this book, and we are grateful to
all of them, but there are a few without whom it just would not
have happened, and to them this book is dedicated.

Thank you—
Hope
Harvest and Spring
George Ulrich and Chas

This book is also dedicated to the memory of

James "Kimo" Cabatbat

who will live on in our memories of this eruption and the many
happy hours we spent at Waha'ula.

In a remote stretch of rain forest on Kīlauea's east rift zone, the
ground ruptured, trees toppled, and soon lava fountains played
above the forest canopy. This was the beginning of the Puʻu ʻŌʻō
eruption in January, 1983, the greatest outpouring of lava on
Kīlauea's flank in this century. For the next three-and-a-half years,
the eruptive activity was episodic, producing forty-seven brief
outbursts of high fountaining. Fallout from the fountains rapidly
built an 835-foot cone, the most prominent feature on Kīlauea's
eastern slope.

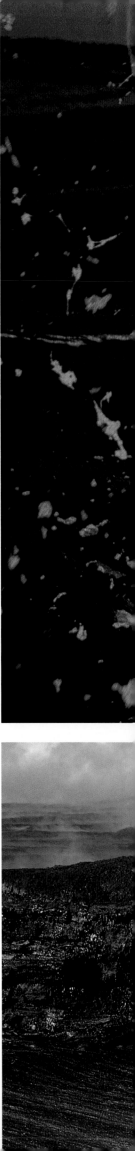

In 1986, the eruption abruptly shifted to a new vent, Kūpaianaha, and a new style of activity. The high fountains were extinguished, replaced by continuous, quiet effusion from a lava pond on top of a broad, low hill of lava.

Kīlauea creates its own art forms. A hollow pillar of lava, formed when lava molded itself around the base of a tree, supports the roof of a glowing cavern in a lava flow only a few hours old.

Few sights are as mesmerizing as a river of molten rock. As flows from Kūpaianaha advanced upon the inhabited coastal area, onlookers were spellbound by the beauty of the lava, as well as by its destructive power.

The lava reached the ocean in late 1986. By 1988, flows poured into the sea almost continuously, and Kīlauea added new land to the island of Hawai'i, a process that has been repeated countless times since the volcano emerged from the sea over a hundred thousand years ago.

Kīlauea
The Newest Land on Earth

"Kīlauea Day Scene" by Titian Ramsey Peale, 1842. Collection of the Bishop Museum.

The History of Kīlauea Volcano

Since the earth's beginnings, volcanoes have brought forth rivers of molten rock from the planet's interior to form new islands, mountain ranges, and vast lava plains. Like most of the processes that shape the earth, volcanism operates on a far grander time scale than the human life span, and few of us ever witness its effects. On the island of Hawai'i, however, human habitation has coincided with an era of volcanic activity that is continually creating new landscapes. The Polynesian immigrants soon discovered they had settled a land that was still under construction, where mountains were literally growing from the sea floor. In the brief interval of historic time, Kīlauea, the island's youngest mountain and one of the world's most active volcanoes, has wrought changes that seem extraordinary to human onlookers. Yet each eruption is only one of thousands of similar events that have gone into the making of the island of Hawai'i.

The earliest written account of Kīlauea's eruptions was made by William Ellis, an English missionary who ascended the volcano on foot in 1823 with three American colleagues and a party of Hawaiian guides. Arriving at the summit, the missionaries looked out over a panorama reminiscent of the fire and brimstone that some members of their calling were wont to invoke. A roiling lake of molten rock lapped the walls of the inner crater, while spatter cones hurled incandescent clots into the sulfurous air. Ellis spent a sleepless night on the edge of the crater, watching the brilliant scene below and questioning his guides about Kīlauea's history. He was told that the volcano "had been burning from time immemorial . . . and had overflowed some part of the country during the reign of every king that had governed Hawaii."

To the missionary's dismay, the Hawaiians professed their belief in the goddess Pele, who made her home in the lava-filled craters of Kīlauea. The tempestuous Pele demanded constant tribute from her subjects, reported his guides, and punished those who neglected her by paying them terrifying visits via her subterranean passageways. Pele's arrival was announced by earth tremors, followed shortly by a flood of lava directed at those who had provoked her displeasure. When a district was threatened by lava flows,

*A party of visiting dignitaries at Halemaʻumaʻu in 1895. The lake has filled
the crater and is contained within levees formed during successive overflows.*

Photograph from the Ray Jerome Baker Collection, Bishop Museum.

*"Astonishment and awe for some moments rendered us mute,
and like statues, we stood fixed to the spot, with our eyes riveted
on the abyss below."*

Rev. William Ellis, the first person to
leave a written record of an eruption at Kīlauea

*An active lava lake occupied the site of the present Halemaʻumaʻu Crater through the 1800s
and into the first two decades of this century.* Photograph by K. Maehara, ca. 1912. Collection of Bishop Museum.

"This inn is a unique and interesting place. Its existence is strikingly precarious, for the whole region is in a state of perpetual throb from earthquakes, and the sights and sounds are gruesome and awful both by day and night."

Isabella L. Bird, an English writer who visited Kīlauea in 1873

The original Volcano House hotel was a small, thatched hut built in 1866.
From the Ray Jerome Baker Collection, Bishop Museum.

By the turn of the century, the Volcano House had become an imposing structure that provided all of the amenities on the brink of an erupting volcano.
Collection of Bishop Museum.

In 1877, the hotel moved into sturdier quarters, which today house the Volcano Art Center. The interior of the main room has changed very little.
National Park Service photograph.

copious offerings to the goddess, usually in the form of pigs, were cast into the lava.

Rituals dedicated to Pele have occurred on Kīlauea since ancient times, though no *heiau* (Hawaiian temple structures) specifically identified with her have survived. The most powerful *heiau* on the volcano was the Wahaʻula Heiau (Temple of the Red Mouth), which endured into modern times on Kīlauea's southern shore. From the fourteenth century until only a few years before Ellis's tour, humans were sacrificed at this site to deities even more demanding than Pele. The ruins of Wahaʻula narrowly escaped destruction in the summer of 1989, when lava flows overran the adjoining National Park visitor center.

Other newcomers to Hawaiʻi followed after Ellis, and Kīlauea soon became a popular stopping place for adventuresome travelers. By 1866, a grass-thatched hotel, the predecessor of the present-day Volcano House, was

prospering on the eastern rim of the summit caldera. One of the first guests was Mark Twain, who noted that "The surprise of finding a good hotel at such an outlandish spot startled me, considerably more than the volcano did." Twain and hundreds of other visitors recorded their impressions of Pele's domain in the Volcano House register, which today provides an important chronicle of the eruption during the last decades of the nineteenth century. The lava lake that Ellis had observed erupted almost continuously during this period, establishing Kīlauea's reputation as one of the world's most active volcanoes.

Scientists were soon drawn to Kīlauea for the same reasons that attracted the early tourists. Here was a readily accessible volcano that was almost

7

"*There is no place on the globe so favorable for systematic study of volcanology and the relationships of local earthquakes to volcanoes as in Hawaii . . . where the earth's primitive processes are at work making new land. . . .*"

Thomas A. Jaggar, first resident geologist at Kīlauea

Thomas A. Jaggar, founder of the Hawaiian Volcano Observatory, observed eruptions from a shelter built on the edge of Halemaʻumaʻu. The small shed at the lip of the crater housed various scientific instruments. U.S. Geological Survey photograph.

The Volcano Observatory was originally located near the site of the present Volcano House hotel. The old hotel is visible in the background. Collection of Bishop Museum.

Thomas Jaggar readies equipment used for analyzing volcanic gases. National Park Service photograph.

constantly erupting yet rarely produced dangerous, explosive eruptions. In 1909, Thomas A. Jaggar, professor of geology from the Massachusetts Institute of Technology, arrived at Kīlauea. Jaggar was a man with a mission. He had witnessed the devastation wreaked by the 1902 eruption of Mt. Pelee, which killed thirty thousand people on the Caribbean island of Martinique, and he was convinced that the only way to prevent similar tragedies was to learn more about the inner workings of volcanoes, preferably at a permanent research station on an active volcano. Jaggar founded the Hawaiian Volcano Observatory in 1912 and zealously nurtured the institution until it was taken over by the U.S. Geological Survey in 1947.

One of the first problems to intrigue the geologists who studied the Hawaiian Islands was that evidence of recent volcanic activity steadily decreased as one moved up the island chain from the southeast to the northwest. James D. Dana, a young geologist who had visited the islands in 1840 with the U.S. Exploring Expedition led by Lt. Charles Wilkes, observed that all of the islands were composed of one or more volcanoes but that on Kaua'i, at the northwestern end of the main island chain, the volcanoes were heavily eroded, thickly vegetated, and long since extinct. The islands appeared progressively younger to the southeast, the youngest being the island of Hawai'i with its active volcanoes.

Dana theorized that the islands had all formed simultaneously and that

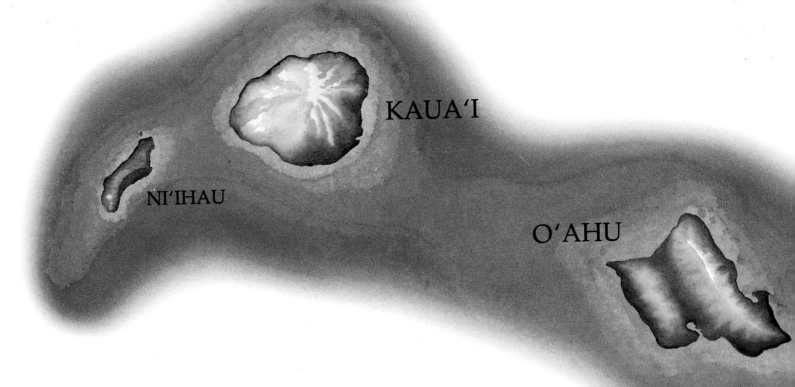

their age progression indicated only the order in which the volcanoes had become extinct. Geologists subsequently determined, however, that the Hawaiian Islands formed sequentially and that the volcanoes do become progressively older to the northwest. The scientists largely confirmed what the Hawaiians had believed for centuries. Ancient legends describe the progression of volcanic activity, telling how Pele moved down the island chain, abandoning each volcano as it grew cold, until she reached her present home in the flaming craters of Kīlauea.

The same sequence is evident on the island of Hawaiʻi itself. The island is made up of five volcanoes, with the oldest, Kohala, occupying the northwest end of the island and the youngest, Kīlauea, the southeast. Deeply eroded Kohala last erupted about sixty thousand years ago, while Mauna Kea, the next in seniority, has been dormant for the last three thousand years. Kīlauea's closer neighbors have both been active within the past two hundred years, Hualalai last erupting in 1800-1801 and Mauna Loa in 1984.

In recent decades, earth scientists have learned that the Hawaiian Islands are the most visible links in a chain of volcanic atolls and seamounts that extends thirty-five hundred miles to the northwest. This chain and the age progression of the volcanoes that form it are explained by the theory of plate tectonics. According to this theory, the earth's crust is divided into a number of rigid plates that shift about on the fluid mantle beneath. Most of the planet's earthquake and volcanic activity occurs at plate boundaries, where adjoining plates either collide or grind past one another.

Hawaiian volcanoes are exceptions to the rule, for they do not owe their origin to the commotion at the plate boundaries. Instead, these volcanoes are forming in the middle of the Pacific Plate as it drifts slowly toward Asia at the rate of a few inches per year. The Hawaiian volcanoes are fueled by a fixed "hot spot" in the earth's mantle, about sixty miles beneath the sea floor. For the past seventy million years, molten rock rising from the hot

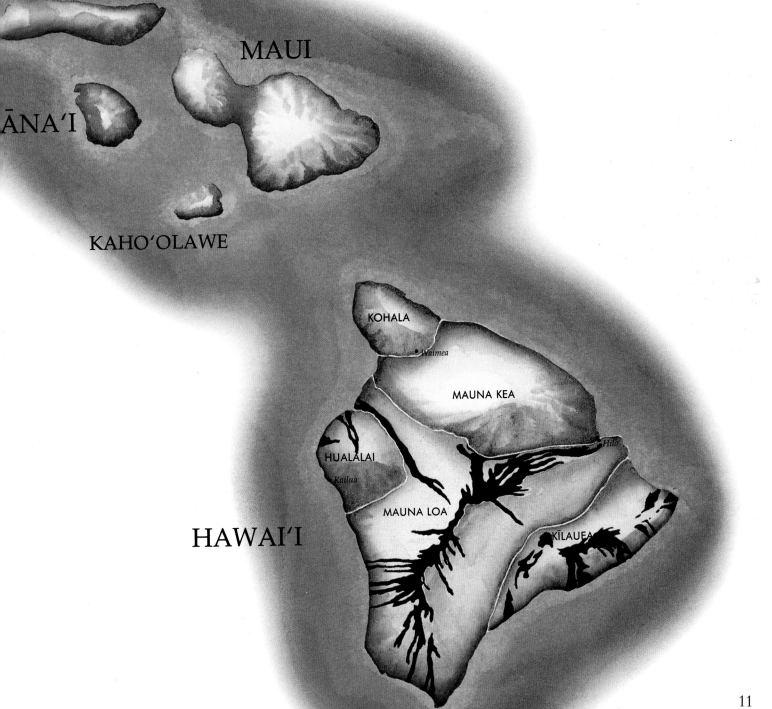

The Hawaiian Islands. Each of the islands is composed of one or more volcanoes. The island of Hawaii consists of five volcanoes, three of which have erupted since 1800. The lava flows from these eruptions are shown in black.

Illustration by Marian Berger.

MOLOKAʻI

MAUI

LĀNAʻI

KAHOʻOLAWE

KOHALA

• Waimea

MAUNA KEA

HUALĀLAI

Kailua

Hilo

MAUNA LOA

KĪLAUEA

HAWAIʻI

Hawaii and the "hot spot." The Hawaiian Islands are formed from molten rock that originated approximately sixty miles beneath the sea floor at a fixed hot spot. The volcanoes rest on the Pacific Plate, which consists of the oceanic crust and the upper layer of the earth's mantle. As the Plate drifts to the northwest, volcanoes are gradually cut off from the magma supply, and new ones begin to grow in their place. The active volcanoes on the island of Hawaii are centered over the hot spot, which is believed to be about two hundred miles in diameter.

Hawaiian volcanoes begin erupting at the bottom of the ocean and must reach a height of almost twenty thousand feet before they breach the waves, a process that takes hundreds of thousands of years. Most of Kīlauea's mass is below sea level, and the weight of the volcano bows the Pacific Plate beneath it.

Kīlauea receives an almost continuous supply of magma from the mantle and stores it temporarily in a shallow reservoir about two miles beneath the summit. As pressure builds in the reservoir, molten rock may rise to the surface and erupt in the summit caldera or it may be diverted to the volcano's flank along one of two long, narrow zones of fractures known as rift zones. This diagram depicts the underground passageway that magma travels through to the site of the latest eruption on Kīlauea's east rift zone. A separate conduit (not shown) leads from the hot spot to Mauna Loa.

Illustration by Marian Berger.

spot has created a long procession of volcanoes as the Pacific Plate has passed overhead. As the Plate drifts to the northwest, each volcano, in turn, is rafted away from the hot spot and gradually becomes extinct. At the far end of the chain, processes of erosion and subsidence eventually cause the oldest volcanoes to disappear beneath the ocean surface.

The southeastern part of the island of Hawai'i, including Mauna Loa and Kīlauea volcanoes, is currently located over the hot spot, along with the newest member of the island chain. Off the southern coast of Kīlauea, still three thousand feet beneath the sea, is a growing volcano named Lōihi, destined to be the next Hawaiian island. Its emergence is not expected for at least ten thousand years.

Besides their origin over the hot spot, several other characteristics set Hawaiian volcanoes apart from their cousins elsewhere in the world. Most important to the scientists who study them, Hawaiian eruptions are generally non-explosive. This mild-mannered behavior can be attributed to the chemical composition of the "magma," which is the term used for molten rock until it reaches the earth's surface. (Thereafter it is called lava.) Most Hawaiian magma is classified as basalt. More fluid than other types of magma, basalt allows much of the gas contained within it to stream upward through the magma and escape harmlessly into the atmosphere. When basaltic magma erupts, it forms long, fluid lava flows. In contrast, the stickier magma of volcanoes such as Mount St. Helens results in explosive eruptions because of the great pressure created by gases trapped within the

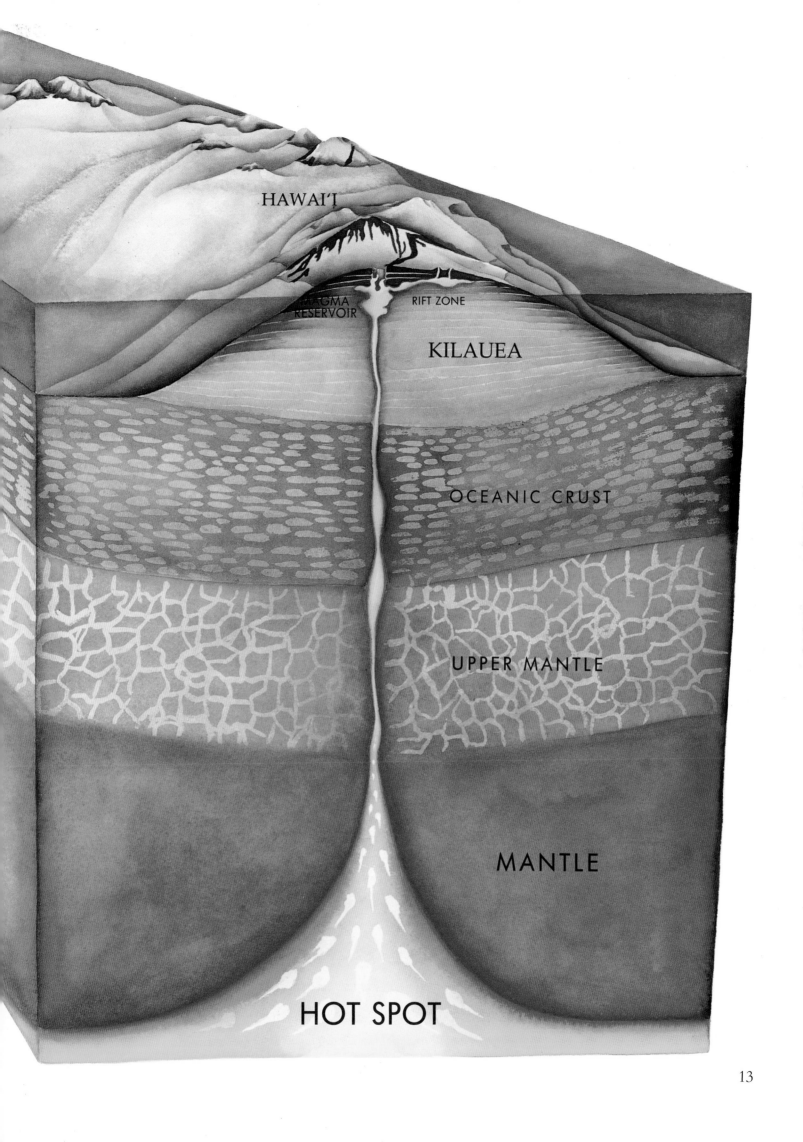

HAWAI'I

MAGMA
RESERVOIR

RIFT ZONE

KILAUEA

OCEANIC CRUST

UPPER MANTLE

MANTLE

HOT SPOT

13

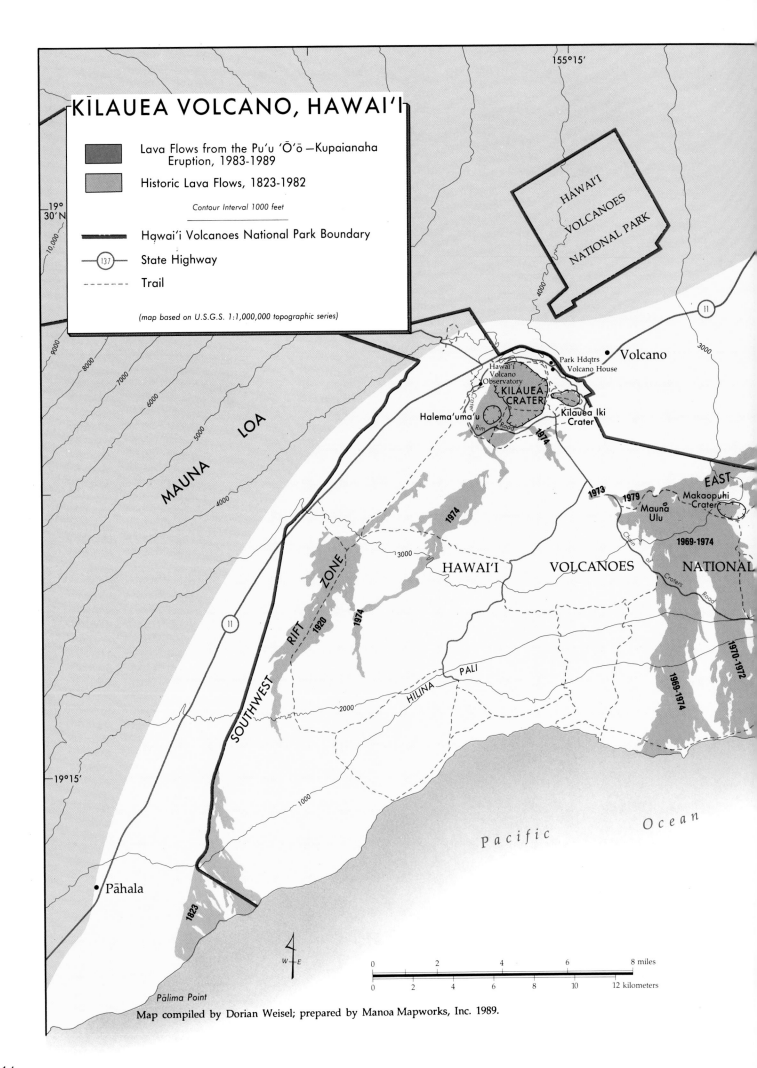

KĪLAUEA VOLCANO, HAWAI'I

Lava Flows from the Pu'u 'Ō'ō —Kupaianaha
Eruption, 1983-1989

Historic Lava Flows, 1823-1982

Contour Interval 1000 feet

Hawai'i Volcanoes National Park Boundary

State Highway

Trail

(map based on U.S.G.S. 1:1,000,000 topographic series)

19°
30'N

10,000

9000

8000

7000

6000

5000

4000

MAUNA LOA

4000

SOUTHWEST RIFT ZONE

1920

1974

3000

HAWAI'I

VOLCANOES

NATIONAL

2000

HILINA PALI

1000

19°15'

• Pāhala

1823

Pālima Point

155°15'

HAWAI'I VOLCANOES NATIONAL PARK

4000

11

3000

Volcano

Park Hdqtrs
Volcano House

Hawai'i
Volcano
Observatory

KILAUEA
CRATER

Halema'uma'u

Kīlauea Iki
Crater

1974

1973

1979

Makaopuhi
Crater

Mauna
Ulu

1969-1974

EAST

Chain

Craters Road

1970-1972

1969-1974

Pacific Ocean

0   2   4   6   8 miles

0   2   4   6   8   10   12 kilometers

Map compiled by Dorian Weisel; prepared by Manoa Mapworks, Inc. 1989.

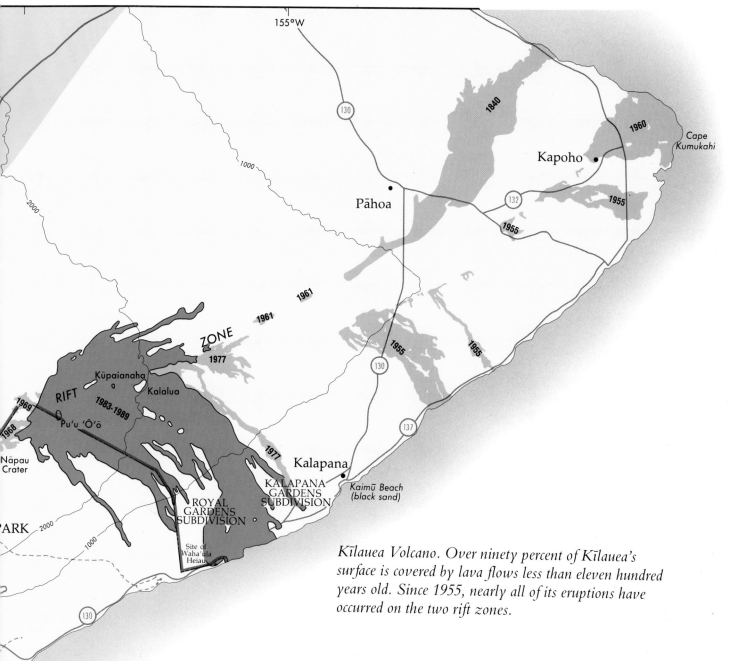

Kīlauea Volcano. Over ninety percent of Kīlauea's surface is covered by lava flows less than eleven hundred years old. Since 1955, nearly all of its eruptions have occurred on the two rift zones.

rising magma. When this type of magma reaches the surface, the pressure is suddenly released, and the gas expands violently, exploding the lava into a boiling cloud of fine ash rather than forming a lava flow.

A Hawaiian volcano in its prime has a distinctive shape, with long, gradual slopes, and a "caldera," or large crater, at its top. The gently-sloping profiles of these volcanoes have earned them the name "shield" volcanoes and are another result of the fluid Hawaiian lava, which flows many miles beyond the eruptive vents. The summit caldera forms by collapse when magma drains away from beneath a vent area following an eruption. Kīlauea's summit caldera is three miles across at its widest point and approximately five hundred feet deep.

Hawaiian volcanoes erupt not only at their summits but also along rift zones, which are heavily fractured zones of weakness within the volcano. Rift zones typically radiate from the summit of the volcano to the ocean and sometimes extend for many miles undersea. Kīlauea has two rift zones: the

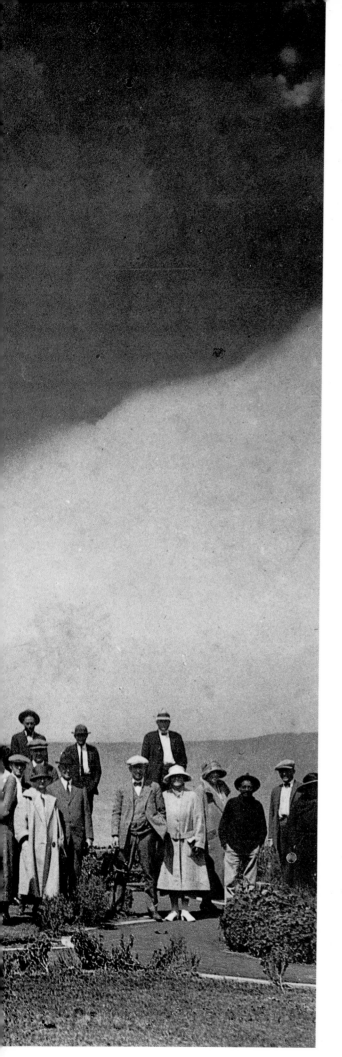

"Uncle George" Lycurgus, proprietor of the Volcano House until his death in 1960 at the age of 101, relaxes in the hotel's library during the 1952 eruption of Halemaʻumaʻu. He viewed many eruptions through these windows after becoming part-owner of the hotel in 1904. *Photograph by Werner Stoy, "Camera Hawaii," courtesy of the National Park Service.*

Spectators pose on the lawn of the Volcano House hotel during the 1924 explosive eruption of Halemaʻumaʻu. *Photograph by Tai Sing Loo. Collection of Bishop Museum.*

east rift zone, which intersects the coastline at Kapoho and continues for about thirty-five miles offshore, and the southwest rift zone, which extends to Pālima Point and ends a short distance beyond.

In historic time, all of Kīlauea's eruptions have occurred in or near the summit caldera or along one of the two rift zones. For over a century after Ellis visited Kīlauea, most of the activity was confined to the site of Halemaʻumaʻu Crater, within the larger summit caldera. This era came to a climax in 1924 with an explosive eruption at Halemaʻumaʻu caused, like all of Kīlauea's infrequent explosive outbursts, by the interaction of water and magma. In the days preceding the explosion, the lava lake had drained away from the crater, and when ground water came into contact with the hot rocks surrounding the magma conduit, the resulting series of steam explosions threw large blocks of dense lava onto the caldera floor. These blocks still litter the caldera near the Halemaʻumaʻu overlook today. One man was killed during this eruption when he ventured to the edge of the crater to take photographs and was struck by a boulder as the next explosion began.

Following the explosive eruption of 1924, sporadic eruptions continued in Halemaʻumaʻu until 1934, when all activity ceased for eighteen years. In 1952, Kīlauea reawoke with another eruption at Halemaʻumaʻu, and for the next 136 days, Volcano House guests were once again treated to pyrotechnics along with their dinner. Although Halemaʻumaʻu has been the site of intermittent activity since then, most eruptions in the past three decades have occurred on Kīlauea's east rift zone.

In 1969, a five-year-long eruption began at the Mauna Ulu vent on the upper east rift zone, producing widespread fields of lava that the Chain of Craters Road now traverses en route to the Kalapana coast. By the time the Mauna Ulu eruption ended, it had set a record as Kīlauea's longest-lived rift eruption in historic time. Yet, in less than a decade, an even more voluminous outpouring of lava was to take place.

The Pu'u 'Ō'ō and Kūpaianaha Eruptions

Shortly after midnight on January 2, 1983, scientists at the Hawaiian Volcano Observatory on Kīlauea's summit were tracking a new wedge of magma as it moved into the volcano's east rift zone. The intruding magma was still two miles beneath the surface of the volcano, but its progress was clearly apparent on the Observatory's seismographs, which record subtle tremors as well as major earthquakes. As the magma forced its way into the rift zone, it fractured the rocks in its path, causing a swarm of small earthquakes. For the next twenty-four hours, the leading edge of the magma could be traced by plotting the earthquake locations on a map.

On the morning of January 3, geologists were camped on the remote lava fields of the rift zone in anticipation of some New Year's fireworks. Pele has a reputation for playing tricks on her admirers, but this time she was punctual. The ground cracked open, sulfurous fumes billowed upward, and lava erupted from the fissures. Newborn rock sprayed from the earth in a long line of fire fountains.

From this point, the eruption became unpredictable, as the magma sought the path of least resistance to the surface. Lava fountains shut off abruptly, only to break out in a new location minutes or hours later. The eruptive fissures cut a swath through the native rain forest from Nāpau Crater to the Kalalua cone, nearly five miles downrift. After three weeks, all activity ceased, and many thought the eruption was over. But in February the eruptive activity resumed, beginning a pattern of episodic eruption that was to last three-and-a-half years.

By June, 1983, the eruption had settled down to a single vent that straddled the eastern boundary of Hawaii Volcanoes National Park. As if to mock any human claims to the ever-changing surface of an active volcano, lava from the new vent rapidly buried the site of a proposed geothermal well field just outside the park. Flows also invaded the Royal Gardens subdivision repeatedly during 1983 and 1984, destroying sixteen houses.

Lava rises from the throat of Puʻu ʻŌʻō with a deafening roar, then falls back to earth to feed the fiery rivers that pour over the side of the cone. The dark particles to the left of the fountain are bits of cooler lava that are carried away by the wind. These cinders rain down on the leeward side of the vent, adding to the bulk of the growing cone.

Two geologists cautiously approach the spattering conduit of Puʻu ʻŌʻō during the interval between high fountaining episodes. The summit of the cone stands well above the conduit because the prevailing northeasterly trade winds have deposited cinders and spatter from the fountains on the downwind side of the vent.

Lava in the Puʻu ʻŌʻō conduit is visible in this photograph at a depth of about one hundred feet. The magma in the conduit, rarely still, churned up and down, emitting hot gases and producing the sound of a gigantic washing machine.

Most eruptive episodes began gradually, with a series of short-lived lava flows, or "spillovers," from the conduit. A spillover begins as upwelling lava engulfs the spatter cone that surrounds the conduit.

The eruptive episodes followed one another with increasing regularity and established a cycle of approximately twenty-six days of repose, followed by thirteen hours of high fountaining. A single, vertical conduit, approximately fifty feet in diameter, fed the towering fountains. At the end of each eruptive episode, the level of the magma in the conduit dropped several hundred feet, then gradually rose during the three-to-four-week period of repose. As the episodes of fountaining became shorter, they also grew more violent, with colossal lava fountains propelling molten rock fifteen hundred feet in the air.

Fallout from these fountains built a cone of cinder and spatter that grew to a height of 835 feet in less than three years. The new cone was soon the most prominent landmark on Kīlauea's east rift zone, and it needed an official name. Hawaiian residents of Kalapana, a community on·the south flank of the volcano, named the new *pu'u* (hill) after the *'ō'ō*, an extinct bird whose brilliant yellow feathers were used in capes and helmets worn by Hawaiian rulers.

On July 18, 1986, after forty-seven eruptive episodes, the nature of the eruption abruptly changed. The vertical conduit beneath Pu'u 'Ō'ō ruptured, and the magma within escaped and ascended to the surface by a new route, breaking the ground as it rose. Soon lava was erupting from fissures at the base of the massive cone. The fissure eruptions ended on July 19 but broke out anew a day later at a site 1.8 miles downrift from Pu'u 'Ō'ō. Here the eruption persisted and another long-lived vent, the successor to Pu'u 'Ō'ō, developed.

At its new location, the eruption no longer adhered to the stop-and-start schedule of high fountaining established at Pu'u 'Ō'ō. Lava spilled continuously and quietly from the new vent with little or no fountaining. Within three weeks, a lava pond had formed over the vent, much like the one that occupied Halema'uma'u Crater in the 1800s. Again the Hawaiians of Kalapana were called upon to bestow a name on Kīlauea's new vent. They chose "*kūpaianaha*," which means "mysterious" or "extraordinary."

After passing the torch to Kūpaianaha, Pu'u 'Ō'ō faded from the spotlight, but even though its tremendous fire fountains were extinguished, possibly forever, geologists were hesitant to pronounce Pu'u 'Ō'ō dead. In June, 1987, the walls of the Pu'u 'Ō'ō conduit, no longer supported by a standing column of magma, began to collapse in a series of events that continued through the following year. By the end of 1988, the collapses had transformed the conduit from a narrow pipe fifty feet in diameter to an enormous crater more than five hundred feet across.

The initial collapses snuffed out a giant flame that had burned over the Pu'u 'Ō'ō vent, fueled by gases released by magma passing beneath the cone on its way to Kūpaianaha. But in late 1987, Pu'u 'Ō'ō began to glow at night more strongly than ever, and when geologists investigated, they discovered that an active lava pond occupied the bottom of the 500-foot-deep crater. The lava pond at Kūpaianaha seemed placid in comparison with the maelstrom in the Pu'u 'Ō'ō crater. Lava in the crater rose and fell in cycles, driven by gases streaming upward through the column of magma to be discharged at its

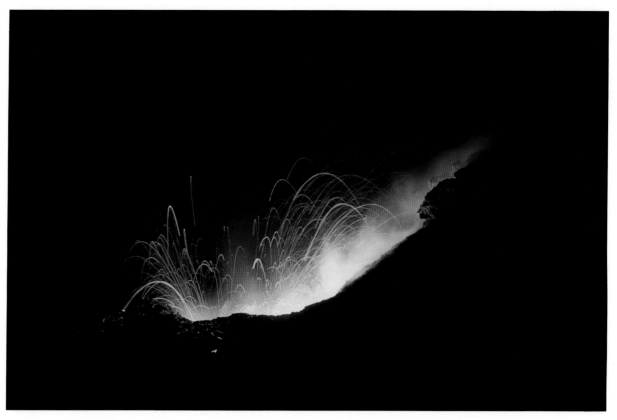

Restless even during periods of repose, Puʻu ʻŌʻō hurls spatter from the glowing conduit.

surface. The new pond was not permanent but came and went throughout 1988 and 1989. At times, only a small pad of sluggish lava covered a portion of the crater floor.

While the activity at the bottom of Puʻu ʻŌʻō waxed and waned, Kūpaianaha continued to erupt without pause. Initially, the lava flows that spilled from Kūpaianaha's quiet pond extended only a few miles from the vent, but this seemingly benign activity was the beginning of the eruption's most destructive phase. The ceaseless effusion of lava from Kūpaianaha soon threatened the communities on Kīlauea's southern coast, as a system of lava tubes gradually developed beyond the margin of the shield. Insulated within the tubes, lava could travel much farther than it could in surface flows before cooling and stagnating, and in three months' time, the tube system extended all the way to the ocean. Flows from Kīlauea reached the sea for the first time in thirteen years on November 28, 1986. The coastal community of Kapaʻahu, which lay in the path of the lava, was rapidly buried.

From December, 1986, through 1989, the lava claimed new territory on either side of Kapaʻahu, briefly invading Kalapana Gardens subdivision to the east and repeatedly encroaching upon Royal Gardens subdivision and Hawaii Volcanoes National Park to the west. More than fifty homes and the Wahaʻula Visitor Center were destroyed, but residents had ample time to evacuate, and no one was injured. Lava flows entered the ocean intermittently during the first half of 1987 and almost continuously from the end of 1987 through 1989, adding over one hundred acres of new land to the island of Hawaiʻi.

With each eruptive episode, Pu'u 'Ō'ō unleashed a force so power-ful that it seemed impossible for the fragile cone to contain it. Here the fountains reach their full height during the night, generating radiant heat that warmed observers more than a mile from the vent.

As the pressure dropped in the local magma chamber below Puʻu
ʻŌʻō, the fountains gradually diminished in size, and the eruptive
episode drew to a close.

During several eruptive episodes in 1986, the last few hours of
fountaining were marked by brief periods of "jetting," when the
fountain became extremely high and narrow for a few minutes then
abruptly died.

Evening mists wreath Puʻu ʻŌʻō, in a scene typical of the middle east rift zone, where a rainforest flourishes in the more than one hundred inches of rain that falls per year. Hot gases have deposited white minerals on the summit of Puʻu ʻŌʻō, giving the cone the improbable appearance of being snow-capped.

On July 18, 1986, a new eruptive fissure opened at the base of
Puʻu ʻŌʻō, and low fountains added a coating of lava to the cinder-
covered landscape.

Lava floods a stand of trees already killed by the frequent barrage of
hot cinders from the high fountains of Puʻu ʻŌʻō.

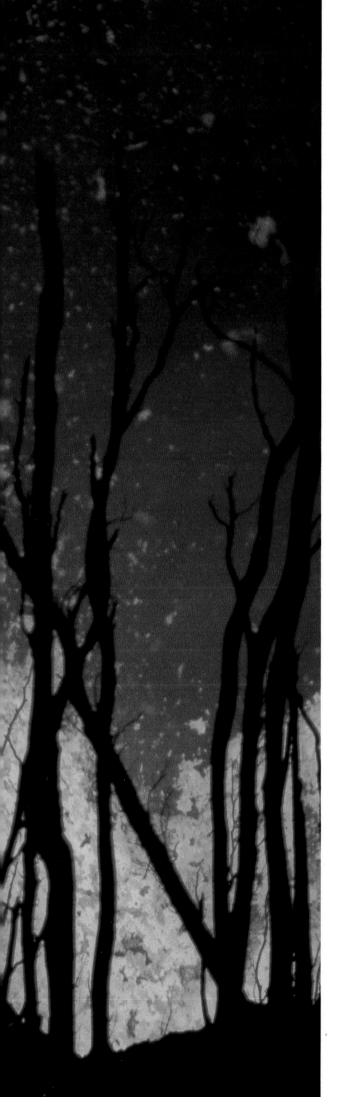

Puʻu ʻŌʻō slumbers against a reddened sky, a blanket of lava wrapped around its base. A fissure eruption on the far side of the cone reflects against the clouds, while a flow from fissures on the near side signals its advance with flashing red lights.

Lava fountains silhouette doomed trees during the July 18th fissure eruption.

Ignited by the heat of the approaching flow, a bush blazes in a cavern left by an older lava flow. The blue flames flickering around the edge of the cavern are from burning gases, including methane, which leak through underground cracks and escape to the atmosphere around the margins of the active flow. If methane is trapped underground, it may explode, heaving rocks and dirt into the air. The muffled booms of methane explosions provide a percussive accompaniment for lava flows advancing through the forest.

On July 20, 1986, lava began spilling from a new fissure almost two miles downrift of Pu'u 'Ō'ō. After three weeks of continuous eruption, a lava pond had formed over the fissure.

The surface of the Kūpaianaha pond is covered with a thin crust that wrinkles and cracks as it is pushed and pulled by the currents in the pond. Lava spatters from a break in the crust at the pond's edge. Pu'u 'Ō'ō stands in the background.

Soon after it formed, the lava pond assumed its distinctive shape, with a long neck leading southeastward from the main part of the pond, which is approximately three hundred feet in diameter.

During the first few months of continuous eruption at Kūpaianaha, most of the lava that entered the pond spilled over its rim, building a broad, low mound called a "lava shield." These two photographs, taken three weeks apart at the same location, show the rapid growth of the shield. In the center foreground is a prehistoric cinder cone that was rapidly engulfed by the expanding shield.

In October, 1986, only the very top of the prehistoric cone remained, an island in a rising sea of lava. Shortly afterward, the cone was submerged forever.

As the Kūpaianaha shield grows, Puʻu ʻŌʻō stands by quietly, eclipsed for now by its more active neighbor.

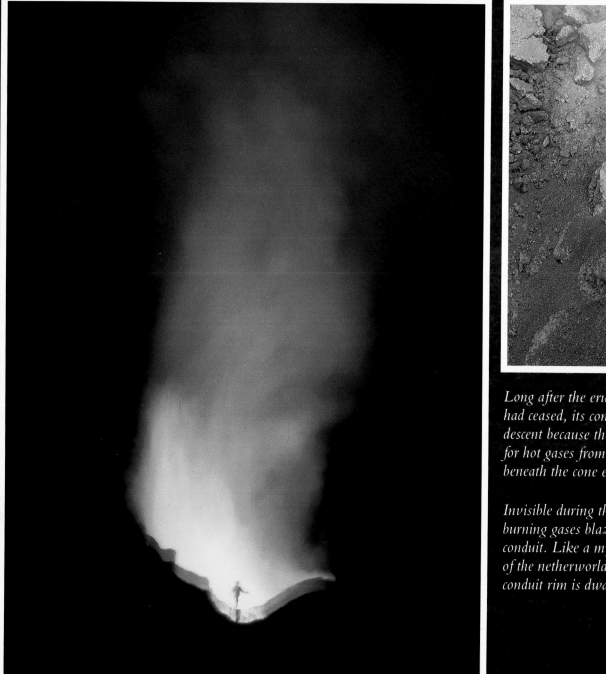

Long after the eruptions at Puʻu ʻŌʻō
had ceased, its conduit remained incandescent because the vent acted as a chimney
for hot gases from the magma passing
beneath the cone en route to Kūpaianaha.

Invisible during the day, at night the
burning gases blazed above the Puʻu ʻŌʻō
conduit. Like a mythical hero at the gates
of the netherworld, an observer on the
conduit rim is dwarfed by the flaring gas.

41

From mid-1987 through 1988, the conduit walls at Puʻu ʻŌʻō repeatedly collapsed, producing a crater more than five hundred feet in diameter. Each collapse was announced by a cloud of reddish rock dust (above) that billowed from the conduit. When one of the largest rockfalls coincided with a torrential winter storm, the plume of dust mixed with rain, and winds deposited the resulting red mud on houses, cars, and vegetation five miles to the north.

At night, Puʻu ʻŌʻō and Kūpaianaha are transformed into beacons visible for miles around. Puʻu ʻŌʻō glows in the distance in this time exposure, while the glare from the Kūpaianaha lava pond illuminates the profile of the lava shield.

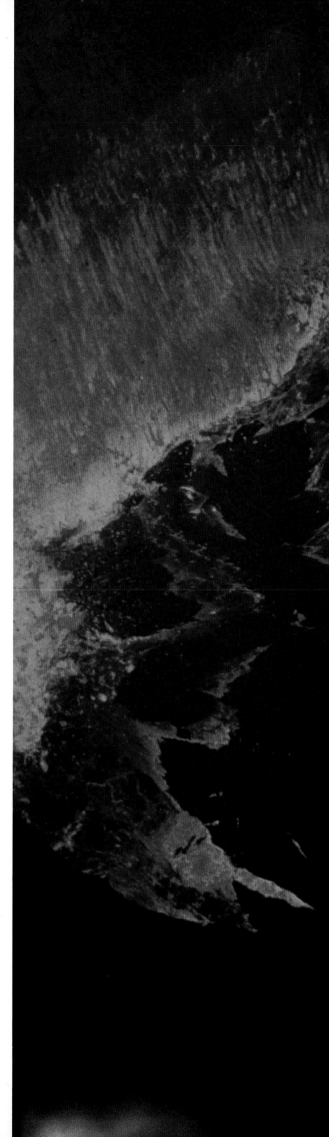

An aerial view, taken from an airplane ten thousand feet above Puʻu ʻŌʻō, shows the well-concealed lava pond in its crater.

On the ground, the Puʻu ʻŌʻō pond is only visible from a precarious perch on the crater rim. The level of the pond has just dropped, leaving behind a high-tide line of glowing lava, clinging to the walls of the crater.

The back wall of the Puʻu ʻŌʻō crater reveals the anatomy of the cone—layers of lava, spatter, and cinders.

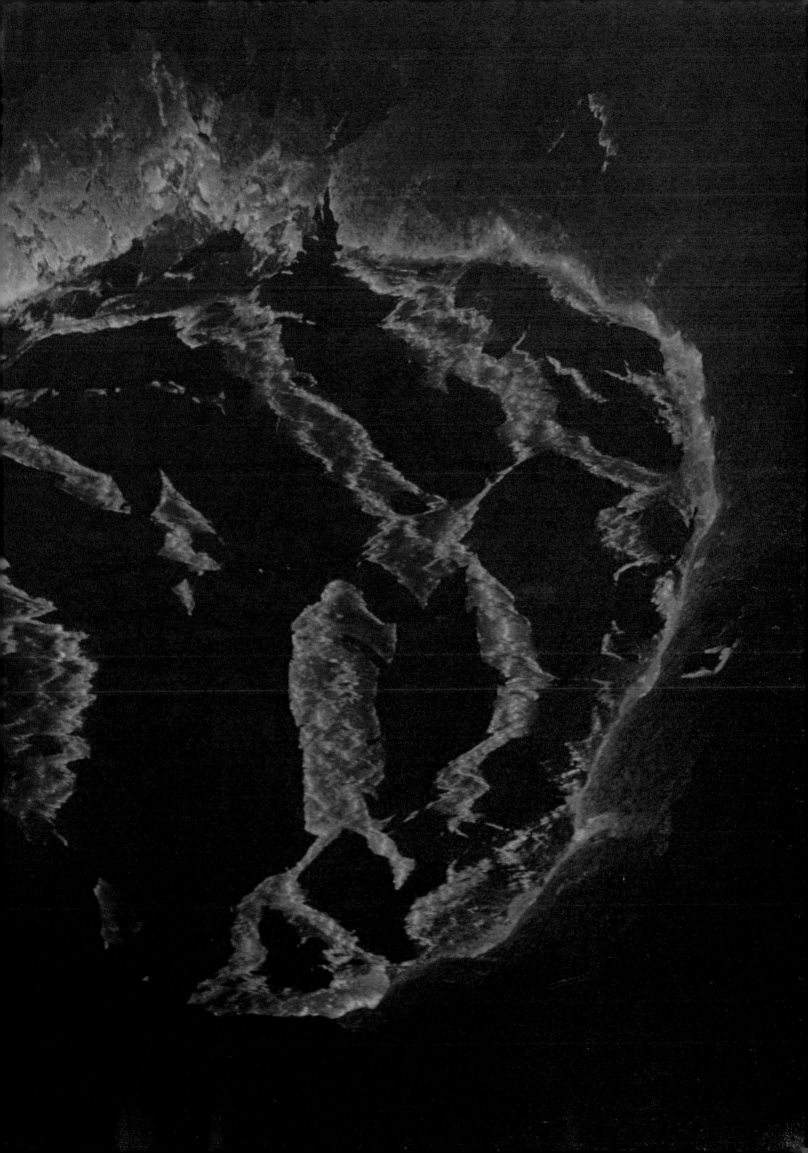

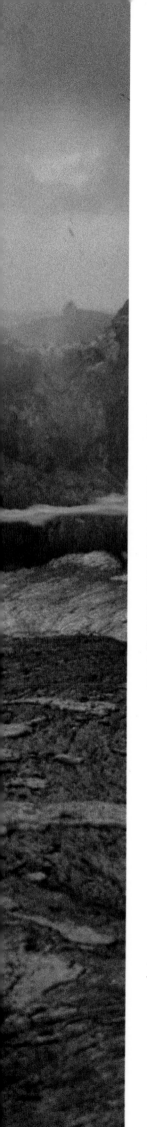

Ever in motion, the lava at the surface of the pond cools and sinks, while hotter lava from the bottom of the pond rises. This circular movement creates convection currents that tear and buckle the crust of the pond and produce an ever-changing pattern of incandescent cracks.

Gas bubbles rise to the surface of the Kūpaianaha pond and burst, flinging out clots of spatter that fall back onto the pond's crust.

A river of lava tumbles over a small cliff on the side of the shield. Kīlauea's lava is approximately 2,100 degrees Fahrenheit when it reaches the earth's surface; the temperature in the interior of an active lava flow is only a few degrees cooler, even after traveling many miles from the vent.

A lava flow spreads out in a broad fan on the east flank of the Kūpaianaha shield, adding to its bulk. The pond is perched on top of the shield in the background.

Hawaiian lava flows can take one of two forms: smooth, fluid pāhoehoe or rough, stickier aʻā. The latter, seen in this close-up view, characteristically has a rubbly surface, which remains sharp, jagged, and inhospitable to travelers after the flow has cooled. The form that the lava takes is determined by the lava's temperature, gas content, and fluidity. A flow that leaves the vent as pāhoehoe may turn into aʻā farther downstream as the lava cools, gives off gas, and becomes increasingly viscous. Flowing over steep slopes can hasten the change from pāhoehoe to aʻā. This change never occurs in reverse.

A large a'ā *flow from Kūpaianaha skirts the forest's edge, covering older flows from the same eruption. The front of the flow is about 150 feet across. Its central, incandescent portion moves most rapidly, while a jagged crust forms at the cooler margins. If the flow maintains the same course for several days, a lava tube may develop, although this process takes place more commonly in* pāhoehoe *flows. Lava tubes form when the crust gradually extends across the entire flow, creating a roof over the central channel and enclosing the flow within a tunnel of its own making.*

A pāhoehoe *flow from Kūpaianaha quietly wends its way through the rainforest. Clinging to life, the native hardwoods are still standing, though their trunks are immersed in a molten tide. One by one, the trees will topple during the next few days as their trunks char through, leaving tree molds in the newly formed rock.*

The leading edge of a pāhoehoe *flow typically advances by means of many overlapping "toes" of lava that sprout from one another. A thin skin forms on the molten appendages as soon as they come in contact with the air. As the lava within the toe continues to flow, the flexible skin is stretched and squeezed into intricate patterns of wrinkles and folds that are preserved as the lava cools. After hardening, a pāhoehoe flow has a smooth, glassy crust and is usually flat or billowy in form. Even before the flow stops advancing, the crust is thick enough for geologists, equipped with heavy boots, to walk on.*

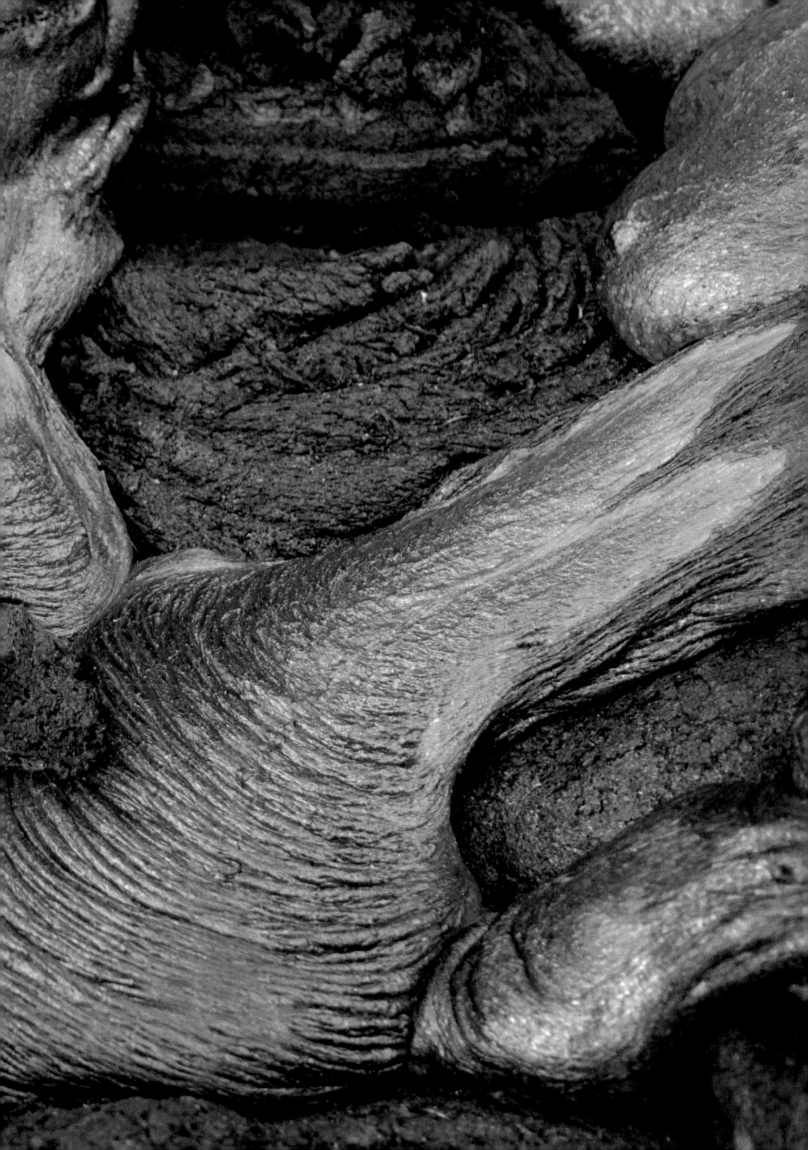

In the autumn of 1986, the growth of the Kūpaianaha shield slowed because the pond was overflowing less frequently than in the preceding months. Most of the lava was now draining from the pond through a lava tube that began at the end of the pond's narrow neck. Fumes rise from the lava tube, just beyond its entrance.

Downslope from the pond, the course of Kūpaianaha's tube system can be traced by a line of fumes, where gases from the underground lava river escape to the surface.

By December, 1987, the neck was completely sealed over, substantially reducing the size of the pond. The photographs on the next two pages show the intermediate stages of this process.

Once the tube system was well-established, the pond overflowed only for brief intervals when the tubes became blocked. The infrequent overflows served to flush away the stagnant crust that accumulated around the edge of the pond. During the last half of 1987, however, the tubes remained open, and no overflows occurred at all. As a result, the ledges of crust slowly formed a roof over the narrow neck of the pond, which eventually became an extension of the main lava tube. Photographs taken in September and October, 1987, show the roof formation in progress.

At twilight, the entrance to the main tube forms a glowing cavern on the far wall of the Kūpaianaha pond.

Skylights form when a section of the lava tube roof collapses. A skylight just beyond the Kūpaianaha lava pond (below) reveals the molten river deep within the shield.

Four miles from Kūpaianaha, lava courses its way underground toward the sea, visible only through a skylight (right). The cloud of steam in the background rises from the point where lava is entering the ocean.

A skylight opens into a world of unimaginable heat. The walls of a
lava tube, glowing in shades of red, are close to their melting point.
The yellow torrent of lava on the floor of the tube radiates enough
heat to scorch onlookers, who can safely approach skylights only
from the upwind side.

This aerial view, taken in 1988, shows destruction caused by lava from the two main vents of this eruption. Flows from Kūpaianaha have paved a thoroughfare extending from Kīlauea's east rift zone to the ocean; a column of steam marks the point where the lava tube empties into the sea. To the left, lava flows from Puʻu ʻŌʻō cut across the streets of the Royal Gardens subdivision. Above the steep slope of the subdivision, gas plumes rise from the Puʻu ʻŌʻō and Kūpaianaha vents. The threat of inundation by lava still hangs over the village of Kalapana, in the lower right corner. Kīlauea's lofty neighbors, Mauna Loa and Mauna Kea, loom in the background.

Piles of metal roofing and abandoned vehicles embedded in the lava are the only evidence that people once lived at Kapaʻahu.

Beyond the power of human intervention, lava consumes a building in the National Park.

Lava crosses Highway 130 as firemen stand by, ready to fight brush fires. By 1989, lava flows from Kūpaianaha had buried two miles of the coastal highway.

In the midst of destruction, the advancing lava sometimes creates strangely peaceful scenes such as this—a flow quietly entering a shallow pool just inland of the ocean. At such moments, it is difficult to imagine the drastic and permanent changes that the lava will bring. Within a few months, the pools and vegetation were gone, and the area had become a desolate plain of pāhoehoe.

Lava tubes disgorge into the surf, generating small steam explosions. The dark lava flows in the background overran parts of the Royal Gardens subdivision during eruptive episodes at Puʻu ʻŌʻō.

A lava tube swallows a mouthful of water and coughs it up explosively in this sequence. The surf breaks over an unroofed portion of the lava tube as the lava stream descends into a tube that drops off steeply into deep water. A ball of water is trapped by an eddy in the descending lava. A few seconds later, an explosion occurs offshore as the trapped water flashes to steam and blows a hole in the underwater tube.

An explosion at the water's edge hurls spatter back onshore, where
it will add to a small cone formed from many such explosions.
These cones are usually short-lived, soon collapsing or succumbing
to high waves.

A small explosion is reflected in the surf at dawn. An enormous
plume of steam rises in the background, where a much larger flow is
pouring into the ocean as Kīlauea continues to create the newest
land on earth.

"Only a Pompeii and a Herculaneum were needed at the foot of Kīlauea to make the story of the irruption immortal."

Mark Twain, *Roughing It*

DORIAN WEISEL, a resident of the island of Hawai'i for ten years and of Kīlauea itself for the last five, conceived and photographed *Kīlauea: The Newest Land on Earth.* He has a special use permit from Hawaii Volcanoes National Park that allows him access to the eruption site in exchange for documenting the volcanic activity on film. A noted freelance photographer, Dorian has shown his work in Honolulu and at the Volcano Art Center and has published photographs in numerous books and periodicals. A selection of his Kīlauea photographs has been included in the major Smithsonian exhibit "Inside Active Volcanoes."

Photograph by Stephen Lang.

CHRISTINA HELIKER is a geologist at the Hawaiian Volcano Observatory. Her career in volcanology began with the catastrophic eruption of Mount St. Helens in 1980, which prompted her to abandon a job studying glaciers and join the team of U.S. Geological Survey scientists at Mount St. Helens. She moved to Hawai'i in 1984 and has been monitoring the Pu'u 'Ō'ō eruption ever since.